The World of Little Muslims

This book belongs to:

_____

In the Name of God, the All-Merciful, the All-Compassionate

The World of Little Muslims

written by
Huwaida Can

illustrated by
Basma Hosam

designed by
Betül Karatay

2020

Published by Tughra Books

335 Clifton Ave., Clifton,

NJ, 07011, USA

www.tughrabooks.com

The World of Little Muslims

Written by Huwaida Can

Illustrated by Basma Hosam

Designed by Betül Karatay

Table of Contents

Glossary

LESSON KEY

Reading

Group Work

LESSON KEY

Brainstorming

Worksheet

About the book

"The World of Little Muslims" is for educators who follow an Islamic education program for young learners.

This book aims to familiarize young minds with the teachings of Islam with a content that focuses on the basics of belief, practice, moral conduct, and etiquette of daily life, and provides numerous stories and hadiths to reinforce the learning process.

Based on an interactive approach, the book is filled with colorful and engaging activities at the end of each lesson.

Chapter 1

ALLAH

Lesson 1   Who Is Allah?

Let's think

- Have you ever seen a star shining in the night sky?
- What has Allah created?
- Who made your eyes?
- Who made this world?
- Who made the Earth as a home for all living things?

◖ VOCABULARY ◗

Allah

SubhanAllah

Al-Khaliq

Who made this world?

"Allah" is the Arabic word for God.
It means: The one God we worship

When we look at the Earth,
the sky, animals, people, we know that
they were created by Allah.

ALLAH

The Creator

Al-Khaliq

He created the Earth
for us to live on.

He created the Sun
to give us light.

He created the Moon
to give us light.

Say
سُبْحَانَ الله

When you see something beautiful,
it means "Glory to Allah" or "Glory be to Allah."

REMEMBER

When you see
pretty flowers and plants,
be careful
not to ruin them.

Enjoy their beauty.

SAY
"SUBHANALLAH"

COLORING

Color the page, and draw some animals.

Write the missing letters. Then write the meaning of the word.

A_L_H

Meaning:

Color the word

Matching

Write the correct letter in front of each word.

 A

 B

 C

 D

 E

 F

Sun ....   Tree ....   Fire ....

Moon ....   Leaf ....   Rain ....

HOMEWORK

* What should we do when we see a beautiful flower? Write it down.

* What is the Arabic word for Allah that means "The Creator"?

Lesson 2   Allah's Favors

Let's think

- What are your favorite fruits?
- How do we know that Allah loves us?
- Why should we love Allah?

VOCABULARY

Allah's gifts

Alhamdulillah

Allah gives us so many gifts,
because He cares about us.

He gives us eyes
to see everything around us.

He gives us a nose
to smell.

He gives us a mouth
to eat.

He gives us ears
to hear.

19

He knows what is best for us, because He is our Creator.

He gives us a family.

He gives us water.

He gives us friends
to play with.

Allah helps us make many useful things.

He gives us wood and metals
to make houses and cars.

He gives us cotton
to make clothes.

WATER

Allah gives us water to drink and clean ourselves.

We all need water to live.

Allah gives us everything we need to live.

Allah gives us homes.

Allah gives us the soil to grow plants.

Allah gives us friends and family.

Allah gives us a lot of gifts, because He loves us.
He gives us the five senses.

Cut and paste.

We .... with our

We .... with our

We .... with our

We .... with our

| eat | sea | hear | smell |

COLORING

Color these delicious fruits that Allah gives us.
Do not forget to say *Alhamdulillah.*

Let's think:

Why should we be thankful?

How do we thank Allah?

Vocabulary:
ALHAMDULILLAH

Thank You
Allah
الحمد لله

Why should we be thankful?

I am thankful to Allah, because:

- He loves me.
- He gives me everything.
- He made me a Muslim.
- Being grateful = countless blessings and finally Jannah in the hereafter.

If you are grateful, I will surely give you more and more.
(Ibrahim 14:7)

How do we thank Allah?

Alhamdulillah means "all thanks are to Allah." We are thankful to Allah because He gives us all we have and He is the most compassionate.

Some ways to thank Allah:

- Say Alhamdulillah and make dua.
- Take care of yourself.
- Pray on time.
- Remind yourself of the favors which Allah gives us.

27

We can never count Allah's blessings, because they are so many!

Be grateful to Allah for everything:
for your life, for your health, for your mind...

Name some things that Allah has given us to be thankful for:

How do you thank Allah?

Chapter 2

THE PROPHET

Lesson 1 The Prophet's Birth

Let's think

- What was his name?
- When was he born?
- What is the Year of the Elephant?

VOCABULARY

Muhammad (pbuh)

Mecca

His name is Muhammad (pbuh).

He was born in Mecca on a Monday,
in the month of Rabi' al-awwal,
in the year 571.

Year of the Elephant

Way back when the Arabs had no official calendar,
they used to name years after special events
that happened in that year.

The year our Prophet Muhammad (peace be upon him) was born, a
really greedy King ruled a city not far from Mecca.
His name was Abraha, and he wanted everyone to visit his city.

The King noticed how most of the people were visiting the Kaaba
which was located in the city of Mecca. He was not happy,
so he built a big, splendid church that would get everyone's attention.

Year of the Elephant

Abraha's plan of gaining more visitors did not work.
People still visited the Kaaba in great numbers.
This made him very angry. So, the mad King decided to
destroy the Kaaba in order to get the attention he wanted.

Abraha created a big army to attack Mecca.
In front of the big army he placed a big elephant from
Africa, named Mahmud. He thought this giant animal would shock
the people of Mecca, for they had never seen elephants before.
Abraha was also going to use the big elephant
to destroy the Kaaba.

Year of the Elephant

However, his plan did not work. Allah did not allow the greedy King to destroy this sacred place. First Mahmud, the Elephant, refused to go ahead towards Mecca. He sat down and nobody could move him.

Second, the Creator of all things destroyed Abraha's army by sending birds, which we call the birds of Ababil.

These birds carried rocks and pebbles in their beaks
to destroy the king's army by dropping them on their heads.
Thus, the year of the elephant was named the year our Prophet was born.
This year show the importance of Allah's power
and the danger of being greedy.

34

ACTIVITY

Connect the right boxes together

Monday, in Rabi' al awwal	because people visited Mecca
Abraha was angry	Our Prophet's name
Muhammad (pbuh)	The Prophet (pbuh) was born on

Fill in the blanks

⭐ Abraha sent an .... to destroy the ....

⭐ The Prophet (pbuh) was born in ....

READ

Day 1 from
"365 Days with the Prophet Muhammad" book
Day 2 is H.W

35

Books:

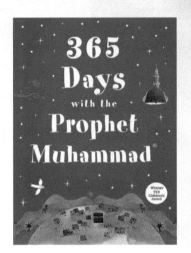

Lesson 2   The Prophet's Family

Let's think

- Who was his mother?
- Who was his father?
- Who was his grandfather?

- Prophet's mother's name was Aminah.
- Prophet's father's name was Abdullah.
- Prophet's grandfather's name was Abdul-Muttalib.

VOCABULARY

Aminah

Abdullah

Abdul-Muttalib

The Prophet's Family

The Prophet's father's name was Abdullah. A few months before the birth of Prophet Muhammad (pbuh), his father Abdullah had gone to Syria with a trade caravan. On his return he fell sick. He stayed in Medina to get better before he went back to **Mecca**.
But sadly he could not reach **Mecca**.

He died in Medina months before the birth of his son.

When his mother Aminah gave birth to him, his grandfather Abdul-Muttalib named him Muhammad. Abdul-Muttalib hoped that his grandson would be praised and respected by everyone in the world.

Let's think

What was the Prophet's grandfather's name?

What was the Prophet's father's name?

What was our beloved Prophet's name?

Trace & Write

READ

Day 3 from
"365 Days with the Prophet Muhammad" book
Day 4 is H.W

Halima, Nursing Mother

In Mecca, the weather was extremely hot. Babies could not survive in the hot temperatures. So, the new born babies were usually sent to another family in a different location with more fresh air and to learn the pure Arabic language. The mother and grandfather of the Prophet Muhammad (pbuh) were looking for a nursing mother to care for our beloved prophet. None of the nursing mothers who came to Mecca wanted little Muhammad (pbuh), because he did not have a father and his family was poor. Halima as Sa'diyyah was one of those nursing mothers who came to Mecca with her husband. But the animals they rode were very weak, so they came very late. The only baby that was left for her was Muhammad (pbuh), so she agreed to take him. But the problem with Halima was that she could not even produce enough milk for her own baby. To her surprise, when she accepted our Prophet and nursed him, her milk was more than enough to feed both babies! Halima realized there was something very special with this baby. When they left Mecca, the animals they rode moved much faster than before. Prophet Muhammad (pbuh) spent his first few years with Halima as Sa'diyyah and her family.

READ

Day 5 from
'365 Days with the Prophet Muhammad' book
Day 6 is H.W

40

Find these words in the grid.

Muhammad , Halima , Medina, Abdullah, Amina

M	K	B	v	c	X	M	z	s	M	u	H	A	M	M	A	D	M
F	G	H	A	J	K	L	K	Q	w	E	R	L	T	y	u	K	N	O
B	X	c	v	A	B	A	K	M	A	B	s	D	F	H	G	H	c	K
A	B	D	u	L	L	A	H	L	Q	H	A	L	I	M	A	H	L	E
M	E	D	I	K	A	H	H	K	I	U	Y	A	M	I	N	A	f	Y

 Who is Halima as Sa'diyyah?

Draw a desert.

Lesson 3   The Prophet's Friends

Let's think

- Do you know our Prophet's friends? Who are they?
- What do we call his friends?
- What did they do for him?
- What does Caliph mean?

VOCABULARY

Sahaba

The Sahaba were from different places, but all of them believed in Prophet Muhammad (pbuh).

They helped the Prophet (pbuh) to spread Islam.

"My companions are like stars, whichever of them you take as a guide, you will be rightly guided."

Ali

Abu-Bakr

* As-Siddiq: the truthful one
* the first man to accept Islam

* the first child
  to accept Islam

Umar

ibn al-Khattab

Uthman

* Al-Farooq
  (The one who distinguishes
  between right and wrong)
* Great debater and wrestler

* The one who put
  all the Quran together
  as a book.

43

Homework

- What do we call the friends of our Prophet?
- Name some of the caliphs.
- What does Al-Farooq mean?
- Read the story of Umar ibn al-Khattab.

READ

Day 7 from
"365 Days with the Prophet Muhammad" book
Day 8 is H.W

STORY
Umar ibn al-Khattab and the poor woman

Umar was one of our Prophet's friends, which we call Sahaba. Umar (ra) was a kind and thoughtful man, and he became the Caliph (the ruler) after Abu Bakr (ra). He always tried to make sure that no one in the city would go to sleep with an empty stomach.

One night, he was walking in the streets to see if there was anyone in need of help. Then as he turned a corner he saw a house where lights were not put out yet. He heard weeping children.

Umar (ra) went to the house and knocked on the door. The mother opened it. Umar (ra) asked her why the children were crying. She said they were hungry. "What are you cooking?" asked Umar (ra).

READ

Day 10 from
"365 Days with the Prophet Muhammad" book
Day 11 is H.W

Umar ibn al-Khattab and the Poor Woman

She told him that she was just pretending to cook food, hoping her children would soon fall asleep. When he saw that there was no food in the pot, Umar (ra) felt guilty. He wanted everyone to have food at their home; but here was a family which was starving. Umar (ra) said to the lady that he would bring food to her right away.

Umar (RA) went to the state treasury. There he put the necessary needs in a big bag and carried it to the lady's house himself. Umar (RA) handed over the bag to the lady. Umar (RA) sat and helped the lady cook the meals.

When the meals were ready the children woke up. As the children ate to their fill they smiled. Umar (RA) felt happy.

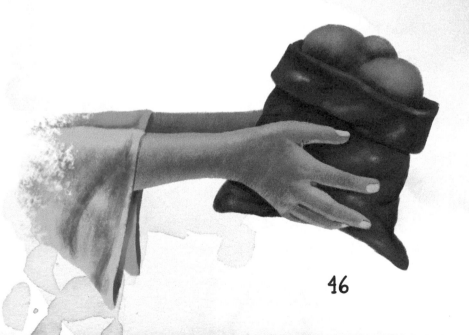

Umar Bin al Khattab and The Poor Woman

Umar (ra) asked the lady why she didn't let the Caliph know about her struggles.

The mother told Umar (ra) that she couldn't beg and ruin her self-respect she had for herself. She argued that the Caliph should have assumed that there were people who were hungry in the city.

Umar (ra) asked her to forgive him. He told her that he would make sure she and her family would no longer be hungry.

When the mother heard that the man who helped her was the Caliph himself, she was happy to see that he was indeed a man of his word.

Homework

- Why were the kids crying?
- Why did not the mom ask for help?
- What can we learn from this story?

Teamwork

Work as a group to discuss the way the family was living at the time and what we should do to help people nowadays.

Lesson 4   The Prophets in the Quran

Let's think

◖ What did I learn from the story?

Prophet Abraham (as)

Story about Prophet Abraham
(as) from "Stories of the
Prophets in the holy Quran" book
*Prophet Abraham (Ibrahim),
the friend of God*

Page 28

READ

Day 12 from
"365 Days with the Prophet Muhammad" book
Day 13 is H.W

49

Prophet Noah

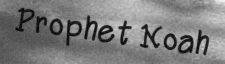

Story about Prophet Noah (as) from
"Stories of the Prophets in the Holy Quran" book
Prophet Noah and the Great Flood
Page 13

READ

Day 14 from
"365 Days with the Prophet Muhammad" book
Day 15 is H.W

Chapter 3

WORSHIP ALLAH

Lesson 1   The Five Pillars of Islam

Let's think

- What does Islam mean?
- What are the five pillars of Islam?
- What does each pillar mean?

◀ VOCABULARY ▶

Islam	Zakat
Shahada	Sawm
Salah	Hajj

Pillars of Islam

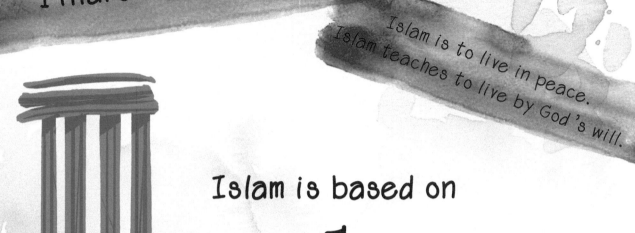

Islam is to live in peace.
Islam teaches to live by God's will.

Islam is based on

5

Pillars

It is based on five very important things that we HAVE TO follow.

What are the Five Pillars of Islam?

1. The Testimony of Faith (Shahada)
2. Prayer (Salah)
3. Support the needy (Zakat)
4. Fasting during the month of Ramadan (Sawm)
5. Pilgrimage to Mecca (Hajj)

3

1

5

Zakat

Testimony

2

4

Pilgrimage

Prayer   Fasting

◖ **1. The testimony of faith (Shahadah)**

The testimony of faith is to say with conviction,

$$\text{لَا اِلٰهَ اِلَّا اللّٰهُ}$$

$$\text{مُحَمَّدٌ رَّسُوْلُ اللّٰهِ}$$

✳ **look over**

"There is no true god (deity) but God (Allah) and Muhammad is the Messenger (Prophet) of God

2. Prayer (Salah)

Muslims perform salah five times a day.

It is a direct connection between the person and God.

We feel happy and relaxed when we pray.

Our Prophet Muhammad (pbuh) said:
"Bilal, call (the people) to prayer, let us be comforted by it."

* Bilal (ra) was a friend of our Prophet. He was chosen to call people to prayers.

3. Supporting the needy (Zakat)

If we are rich enough, it is an obligation for us to
support the needy with zakat.

Zakat is not a gift given out of kindness.
It is a duty to help the poor.

Zakat helps to save ourselves from greed.

Zakat teaches us self-discipline.

Zakat teaches us to behave honestly.

55

4. Fasting the month of Ramadan (Sawm)

All Muslims fast from dawn until sunset, every year in the month of Ramadan.

The fast is beneficial to our health.

5-The pilgrimage to Mecca (Hajj)

The pilgrimage (Hajj) is a visit to Mecca. Every Muslim, who is in good health and can travel, go on the Hajj at least once in their lives.

During the Hajj, pilgrims wear simple clothes and all stand equal before God.

Cut and Paste

1	2	3	4	5
Shahada	Prayer (Salah)	Fasting (Sawm)	Zakat	Hajj

Muslims do this five times a day.	Muslims are expected to do this once in their lives.	Supporting the needy	Eating and drinking nothing from sunrise to sunset	Muslims believe and say there is no god but Allah and Muhammad is His Messenger (pbuh)

Lesson 2   Prayer

Let's think

- How do we pray?
- How many times do we pray?
- In which direction do we pray?
- Why do we pray?

◀ VOCABULARY ▶

Pray

Salah

SALAH

Salah means worshipping Allah with words and actions.
It starts with takbeer and ends with tasleem.
It is the second pillar of Islam.
Young kids at seven are encouraged to pray.

The five daily prayers

Fajr Prayer

Dhuhr Prayer

Asr Prayer

Maghrib Prayer

Isha Prayer

SALAH

When the time of the prayer starts the mu'addhin in the masjid call out the adhan.

We then do wudu (wash parts of our body) and get ready for salah.

We face the qiblah, and make the intention of the prayer we are going to perform.

We raise our hands to the level of our ears or shoulders and say: "Allahu Akbar". And this means our prayer has started.

In each rak'ah we need to do the followings :

1- Recitation of Subhanakah

2- Recitation of Surat AL-Fatihah while standing.

3- Recitation of another surah (in the first two rak'ahs)

4- Ruku': Bowing with our hands on our knees.

5- Sujud: Prostration - done twice (putting hands, forehead and nose, knees and toes on the ground)

Details in how to do each part of the rak'ah will be shown later!

HOMEWORK

Fill out the chart

	Monday	Tuesday	Wednesday	Thursday	Friday	Saturday	Sunday
Fajr							
Dhuhr							
Asr							
Maghrib							
Isha							

My goal is to get .... stars this week.

My reward is ....

READ

Day 17 is H.W. from
"365 Days with the Prophet Muhammad" book

Color the rug

Design and decorate your rug

Lesson 3   Ramadan

Let's think

- Why is Ramadan important?
- Why do people fast in Ramadan?
- What is the Quran?
- What is Lailatul Qadr?

VOCABULARY

Ramadan

Quran

What is Ramadan?

Ramadan is the Holy Month for Muslims.

Ramadan is the ninth month of the Islamic calendar

The Quran was first revealed to our Prophet (pbuh) in Ramadan.

Lailatul Qadr is in Ramadan.

The meal before the beginning of the fast is called suhur,

and the meal after sunset is called iftar.

Our duties in Ramadan

Fasting is one of the most important duties of Ramadan.

Fasting is fard on every healthy adult.

Children don't have to fast.

While fasting, we do not eat or drink from sunrise to sunset.

During Ramadan, Muslims are encouraged to read the Quran

more than at other times.

66

Ramadan word search

Name : ....   Age: ....

fast, worship, suhur, salah, Muhammad, friend, iftar

W	O	R	S	H	I	P	E	R	G	F	A	S	T	L	M	K	Q	U	R
A	N	M	L	P	I	F	T	A	R	W	E	A	S	U	H	U	R	J	K
L	S	A	L	A	H	E	Q	W	S	M	U	H	A	M	M	A	D	E	W
S	R	F	R	I	E	N	D	D	C	Y	M	M	K	L	I	N	B	Y	C

READ

Day 18 from
"365 Days with the Prophet Muhammad" book
Day 19 is H.W.

HOMEWORK

Write the correct answers in the blanks.

1 - We must perform this five times a day and it always requires that you kneel towards Mecca.

....

2 - Muslims take this trip at least once in their life to the holy city of Mecca.

....

3 - "There is no god but Allah, Muhammad (pbuh) is the Messenger of Allah." What do we call this statement?

....

4 - If we are rich enough, it is an obligation for us to support the needy with this.

....

5 - We must do this every year during the holy month of Ramadan.

....

READ

Day 16 from
"365 Days with the Prophet Muhammad" book

Lesson 4   Practicing Sunnah

Prophet Muhammad (peace be upon him) is the last
Prophet of Allah Almighty. Allah gave His
Messenger two sources of wisdom:
the Quran and the Sunnah.

The Sunnah refers to everything that is said, done,
or approved by the Prophet, peace be upon him.

It is very important to know and follow the Prophet's Sunnah.
This is how we can be successful in both worlds.

By following the Prophet's Sunnah we can lead a happy
and healthy life.

Some of the Sunnahs are:

Use of miswak

Miswak is a stick with a soft end.

It is used to clean the teeth.

Always having a pleasant smile

Speaking good or keeping silent

69

Practicing Sunnah

Sunnahs of eating

Before eating, say "Bismillah wa 'la barakatillah"

Eat with the right hand.

Eat from the side that is in front of you.

Recite the dua after eating.

اَلْحَمْدُ لِلّٰهِ الَّذِى اَطْعَمَنَا وَ سَقَانَا وَ جَعَلَنَا مِنَ الْمُسْلِمِينَ

Classwork

Set up a table and eat with the kids.

Ask each child a sunnah to follow.

Homework

Memorize the dua after eating.

70

Sunnahs of drinking

Say "Bismillah" before drinking.

Drink with the right hand.

Drinking while sitting.

Drink in 3 breaths (sips).

After drinking say "Alhamdulillah".

Classwork

Ask each child to drink and follow what they have learned.

Practicing Sunnah

Sunnahs of sleeping

Recite Ayatul Kursi.

Recite 3 times Surah Ikhlaas, Surah Falaq, and Surah Naas into your hands and rub your hands over your body.

Recite the following dua before sleeping.

$$بِسْمِكَ اللّٰهُمَّ اَحْيَا وَاَمُوْتُ$$

Turn to your right.

Place your right hand under your cheek.

Classwork

Set up a bed and show the kids the way we should sleep.

Homework

Memorize a dua before sleep.

Sunnahs when entering the home

Say the dua before entering the home.

Greet your family with "Assalaamu alaykum."

Make others know you have arrived by greeting or coughing, even though it may be your own house.

Classwork

Ask each child to enter the room and follow the sunnah.

welcome

Homework

When you arrive home, greet your family.

Chapter 4

MY MUSLIM WORLD

1   Masjid

2   Holy Places

Lesson 1   Masjid

Let's think

- What does masjid mean?
- How should you behave at the masjid?
- What do we call the person who calls the adhan?
- What does a mosque have inside?

◖ VOCABULARY ◗

mosque

qibla

adhan

masjid

MASJID

The mosque

is a place to gather for prayers, study, and to celebrate religious holidays.

A typical mosque includes a minaret, a dome, and a place to wash before prayers. Each feature has its own significance. In the prayer hall , there is a niche, called the mihraab.

The mihraab

shows the direction of the qibla. The qibla is the direction towards Mecca. When it is time for salah, the mu'addhin calls out the adhan from the masjid.

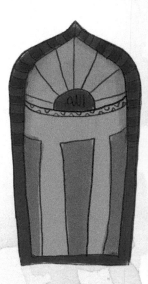

The adhan

is a call for prayer.

Some mosques are small.

Some mosques are huge.

A few things to follow when you enter the mosque:

Take off your shoes or sandals and leave them at the entrance to the mosque. Put them on the shelf if there is one.

Enter with your right foot.

Keep the mosque clean.

Make sure your body and clothes are clean.

Do not eat or drink.

Leave the mosque with your left foot.

Find your way to the mosque:

79

Lesson 2   Holy Places

Let's think

◖ What are the holy places?

◖ **VOCABULARY** ◗

Kaaba

Masjid al-Aqsa

Masjid an-Nabawi

Holy Places

Certain places are important in Islam, for Allah has made them holy. These places were where the Prophet Muhammad (pbuh) lived or visited. They are important for all Muslims.

The holiest place in all of Islam is the **Kaaba** in Mecca.

The Kaaba is the house of Allah. It was built by Prophet Ibrahim (pbuh) and his son Ismail (pbuh) thousands of years ago. They used stones to build the Kaaba.

While building the Kaaba, Ibrahim (pbuh) stood on a rock to raise the walls.

Visitors to Mecca can see this rock at Maqam Ibrahim near Kaaba. The footprints of Ibrahim (as) are also visible on the rock.

Holy Places

The second holy place in Islam is
Al-Masjid an-Nabawi in Medina.
The Prophet Muhammad's home (pbuh) was
next to this Masjid.
His home and the Masjid were built after
his migration to Medina.

The third holy place is
Masjid al-Aqsa
in Jerusalem, which was the original
qibla (direction of prayer)
before it was changed to Kaaba
in Mecca.

Color the page

READ

Day 22 from
"365 Days with the Prophet Muhammad" book
Day 23 is H.W.

ACTIVITY

Visit a mosque in your neighborhood, write your experience.

What is the name of the place where the adhan is called from?

What is the purpose of the mihrab?

READ

Day 20 from
"365 Days with the Prophet Muhammad" book
Day 21 is H.W.

Chapter 5

MANNERS

Lesson 1   Kindness

Our Prophet Muhammad (pbuh) taught us to act with love, kindness, and compassion to other people. We have to support especially the weak and poor people.

Prophet Muhammad (pbuh), peace and blessings be upon him, said, "Every act of kindness is a Sadaqa (charity)." (from Bukhari and Muslim)

Acts of Kindness

When you are in need, ask politely in a mannered fashion.

Each smile counts as charity.

Respect the elderly.

Be attentive and respectful to everyone and everything around you.

Greeting people is a sign of respect.

Show your love to your parents, siblings, friends, and relatives.

HADITH

A man asked Allah's Messenger to
whom he should show kindness the most.
The Prophet replied: "Your mother."

The man then asked: "Who after the mother?"
The Prophet replied: "Your mother."

The man asked the same question again: "Who after
the mother?" The Prophet replied for the third
time: "Your mother."

When the man asked the same question,
the Prophet(pbuh) replied:
"Your father, then your
relatives in order of relationship."
(from Abu Dawud)

The ways of showing kindness to your mother

Do not raise your voice while speaking with her.

Help with the house chores.

Do not display a harsh attitude.

Do your homework.

CLASSWORK

Are you a kind person? Draw a picture and show how.

How do you show kindness to others?

HOMEWORK

ACTS OF KINDNESS AT HOME AND SCHOOL

	Check mark the chart below daily	
MONDAY	Set the table for dinner.	
TUESDAY	Hold the door open for someone.	
WEDNESDAY	Help your friends.	
THURSDAY	Give food to a hungry person.	
FRIDAY	Ask someone how they are doing and listen.	

5 Check marks : ....

Cleanliness

Keeping our surroundings clean is important.

Caring for one's hygiene is a good
habit. It is a part of the faith, too.

Personal hygiene

Brush your teeth.

Take bath.

Take care of your hair.

Wash your hands.

Wash and wipe after
using the toilet.

HOMEWORK

Fill out the chart with and bring it back next week.

Day \ Action					
MONDAY					
TUESDAY					
WEDNESDAY					
THURSDAY					
FRIDAY					

10 😊 : ....

15 😊 : ....

Lesson 2   In the Bathroom

Our religion Islam teaches even how to act in the bathroom,

so we can stay clean and healthy.

Here are some rules to follow:

1-You should go to the bathroom as soon as you need to.

2-Enter the toilet with your left foot and say:

$$اَللّٰهُمَّ اِنِّي اَعُوذُ بِكَ مِنَ الْخُبْثِ وَالْخَبَائِثِ$$

3-Use water to make sure you properly

clean yourself after using the bathroom.

In the Bathroom

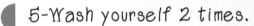

- 4-Sit on the seat.
- 5-Wash yourself 2 times.
- 6-Flush the toilet.
- 7-Wash your hands and wipe them dry.
- 8-Leave the bathroom with your right foot and say:

غُفْرَانَكَ

Homework

Study the dua for entering and leaving the toilet.

Lesson 3   At the Table

HADITH

"Mention the name of Allah and eat with
your right hand and eat of the dish
nearer you"
(from Bukhari)

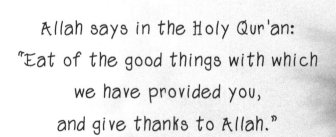

Allah says in the Holy Qur'an:
"Eat of the good things with which
we have provided you,
and give thanks to Allah."

What to follow

بسم الله الرحمن الرحيم

1- Make sure what you are eating is Halal.

2- Wash your hands.

3- Say **Bismillah** before you start eating.

4- Eat with your right hand.

5- Make sure your plate is close to you.

6- Never talk with your mouth full.

7- If the food is too hot, wait until it cools down.
Do not blow on the food.

8- Always finish all the food on your plate.

9- Do not over eat.

10- Put a little food on your plate and add more if you are still hungry.

11- When you are done eating say **Alhamdulillah**.

12- Finally, wash your hands and mouth.

حلال Halal

HOMEWORK

Write the correct answers in the blanks:

1- Before you start eating you should _____ your hands.

2- You should wait for the food to _____

3- You should not eat _____ food.

4- When you have finished you should say _____
and _____ your hands.

Classwork

Set up a table and eat with the kids.

Lesson 4   Honesty

HADITH

"Truthfulness leads to righteousness and righteousness leads to paradise."
(from Bukhari)

Honesty was one of the characteristics of the Prophet (peace be upon him). He was called al-Ameen, which means "thetruthful and the trustworthy."

READ

Day 24 from
"365 Days with the Prophet Muhammad" book
Day 25 is H.W.

How should we understand honesty?

Honesty

Sincerity

Trust

Commitment

Reliability

Some tips to be an honest person:

- If you are in school, do not cheat in any way. Cheating does not lead to success.
- If you are working, be honest in your job, giving a full amount of work for your pay.
- Do not rationalize dishonest behavior.
- Do not make commitments that you are not sure about. But if you make a commitment make sure you carry it out.
- Do not make up stories to make yourself look better.
- Accept mistakes and be ready to face the consequences.
- People who feel good about themselves are less likely to lie.
- Avoid situations in which others may ask you to lie for them.

CLASSWORK

Write the correct answers in the blanks:

1 - Every act of kindness is a ....

2 - Our Prophet Muhammad (pbuh) taught us to act with .... ,
.... , and .... to other people.

3 - Do not ....towards parents.

4 - Friends should take turns and ....

5 - Always do your .... at school.

6 - It is important to be ....

7 - Put a .... on your face.

Word bank:

smile	share	helpful	kindness	be disrespectful
best	sadaqa	love	compassion	

HOMEWORK

Write 1 thing that shows your honesty.

Why is it important to be an honest person?

Find the words in the grid:

honest   trust   commitment   al-Ameen

A	L	S	P	O	H	O	N	E	S	T	P	L
L	K	M	T	R	U	S	T	B	Y	F	X	I
C	O	M	M	I	T	M	E	N	T	M	M	J
A	L	A	M	E	E	N	O	A	U	Y	T	R

Lesson 5   Modesty

Modesty plays a crucial part in Islam.

Being modest helps us avoid acting improperly or indecently in our lives.

HADITH

Prophet Muhammad (pbuh) once said:
"Faith consists of more than seventy branches.
And haya (modesty) is a part of faith."
(from Bukhari)

Modesty strengthens worship and obedience to Allah.
We must also be truthful, sincere, humble, patient,
forgiving, charitable, moderate, kind, and considerate.

Modesty for women and men

Women:

As a sign of modesty, women wear hijab, and they do not reveal their legs, arms, and stomach.

Men:

Men cover their heads during prayer.
They do not reveal their legs and stomach.